RISING ABOVE DEPRESSION

Embracing Emotional Well-Being: A Guide to Navigating Life's Challenges

BY

Stella C. lane

TABLE OF CONTENTS

INTRODUCTION

An essential component of human conduct is how ideas and deeds interact. Our thoughts serve as the building blocks for our behaviors, and they precede our acts. The degree to which ideas prevail over deeds, however, might change based on a number of variables, including our self-control, values, emotions, and outside influences.

Strong emotions, such as wrath or fear, can sometimes overwhelm reasonable thought and lead to rash behavior. Individuals may, however, learn to control their emotions and make decisions that are in line with their long-term goals by developing emotional intelligence and mindfulness.

Value based questions

1. On your way to work one day, you passed a coworker by. You waved at him, and it was clear that he saw you, but he did not respond. Then, at work, you saw the same

coworker conversing with another person as your eyes locked. What would you think or react to at this point?

2. You had two commercial deals you wanted to enter, and everything had been well prepared, but due to unforeseen events, you could not complete the first contract. Now that your best buddy participated in the first transaction, it was highly profitable. Later, the deal you became engaged with was a failure. And this doesn't appear to be the first time something of this nature has occurred to you. What do you think about this and how would you react to it?

3. You are among the top students in your high school class. You are so intelligent and polite that everyone nearly envies you. You learn that you have the lowest success rate of almost all your high school friends on the day of your reunion. Many of them are doing well on their own, but you are still having a hard time paying your bill each month. What would be your thought and response to this afterward?

4. Your close friends have boyfriends or girlfriends, live freely, go to parties, and carry out their daily activities as

they like. How do you feel about the fact that, in contrast to what your friends have, your parents are literally against all of those things and tell you what to do, when to do it, and how to do it?

Even if the situations described above might not apply to you, how would you respond if they did? If you failed to respond to the above question, please go back and do it.

People does wake up with a number of thoughts every day; some are his daily ambitions, some are unmet goals, some are regrets for previous errors, etc. The way your day goes depends entirely on how you shape your thinking. Affirm to yourself that nothing you will experience today will be worse or better than what you have already seen. When you wake up positive, nothing will overcast you on that day.

When a coworker ignores your welcomes after you make this sort of affirmation, you could think to yourself, "Who knows where his mind is, I'm sure he clearly did not notice even though he is looking at me." When you see him in the workplace, you approach him and strike up a conversation.

Then, when you see your friends surpassing you, you shouldn't feel sorry for yourself; instead, it should prompt you to stop and assess if you are advancing at an appropriate rate and in the proper direction. After that, you should continue living your life to the fullest. If you don't cave in to pressure, nobody has the right to.

In many circumstances, our ideas might really take precedence over our immediate actions. This frequently happens when we practice restraint. For instance, if you're devoted to a healthy diet, you may suppress the want to consume a slice of cake by reminding yourself of your long-term health objectives.

Your ideas are more likely to direct your actions if they coincide with your basic beliefs. On the other hand, if your ideas are at odds with your morals, you can feel conflicted or guilty, which might cause you to behave contrary to what you believe in.

The environment as well as external factors can also affect whether thoughts prevail over behaviors.

Sometimes social pressure, peer pressure, or cultural conventions can cause people to act in ways that are at odds with their beliefs or morals. This is frequently observed in instances of collaborative thinking or conformity.

while thoughts are powerful determinants of our actions, the extent to which they override our actions can vary widely. Developing self-awareness, self-control, and a strong sense of one's values can help individuals better align their thoughts with their actions and make choices that are in harmony with their long-term goals and well-being.

Being able to manage your thoughts is a difficult but important ability that may have a significant influence on your happiness, decision-making, and general sense of fulfillment in life.

Paying non-judgmental attention to your thoughts and feelings while engaging in mindfulness meditation is a very effective technique.

You may gain more awareness and control over your ideas by just watching them without attempting to alter or suppress them.

Regular mindfulness practice can assist you in separating from unfavorable or bothersome ideas and making the decision not to act on them.

Recognize Recurring Thought Patterns: Become conscious of thoughts that tend to repeat themselves, such as negative self-talk, catastrophizing, or ruminating.

Keep a journal to document these mental processes as they occur. The first step in taking control of them is to identify them.

Challenge Irrational Ideas: When you come across negative or illogical ideas, question their veracity.

Ask yourself if there is proof for these beliefs. Are they founded on actual data or suppositions?

Replace unfavorable thoughts with more sensible and uplifting ones.

Establish Time Limits for Worrying: Set aside certain hours of the day for worrying or attending to worries. Try to shift your focus to more uplifting or useful topics outside of these set periods.

Reduce your time spent worrying gradually to lessen the influence it has on your day-to-day activities.

Use Distraction Techniques: When intrusive or useless ideas come to mind, divert your attention with interesting tasks or hobbies.

Physical exercise, artistic endeavors, or simply switching your attention to something else might divert your attention.

Affirmations that are positive might be used to dispel unfavorable ideas. These succinct, affirming remarks might help you change your perspective.

If you are thinking, "I'm not good enough," for instance, change it to, "I am capable and worthy."

Practice Being Grateful: Make a practice of being thankful by constantly thinking back on your life's blessings.

Positive mental patterns may be changed by concentrating on your blessings.

Be Aware of Media, People, or Environments That Consistently Encourage Negative Thought Patterns. Limit Your Exposure to Such Influences. Look for More Positive and Supportive Sources.

Summary of out of depression practices

1. Meet yourself where you are

Millions of individuals, including those in your life, struggle with depression. You might not be aware that they encounter comparable difficulties, feelings, and hurdles.

You may be able to manage depression by being honest, accepting, and caring toward yourself and what you're going through.

2. Consider a walk around the block

Exercise can seem like the last thing you'd want to do on days when you don't feel like getting out of bed. However, physical activity and exercise can boost energy levels and help lessen the effects of depression.

According to research from a reliable source, for some people, exercising can help with depression symptoms just as well as taking medication. Additionally, it could help stop future depressed episodes.

See whether you would be willing to do the opposite of what your mood tells you to do, even when you feel like you can't or don't have much energy. Set a more modest objective for yourself, like going for a short stroll around the block.

3. Be aware that today doesn't always foretell future.

Day to day variations in internal feelings and ideas are possible. You can keep track of experiences by writing or by maintaining a mood journal.

If you have trouble getting out of bed or achieving your goals today, keep in mind that you still have tomorrow to try again.

Allow yourself the luxury of understanding that while some days will be challenging, other days will also be less challenging. Try to anticipate tomorrow's new beginning.

4. Evaluate the components rather than assuming the whole.

Recollections might be colored by painful feelings due to depression. You could realize that you're concentrating on issues that are challenging or seen as being ineffective. Stop trying to generalize too much. Strive to focus on the positive. If it helps, make a list of the significant aspects of the occasion or day. You may keep track of your daily accomplishments and the fun activities you engaged in. You might be able to shift your focus to the specific parts that were useful by realizing how much weight you're putting to one thing rather than the total.

5. Take the opposite action to what your "depression voice" advises.

Your inner voice could discourage you from seeking self-help. But if you can learn to identify this voice, you can figure out how to deal with it.

If you doubt that anything will be enjoyable or worthwhile, tell yourself, "You might be right, but it'll be better than just sitting here another night." Eventually, you could realize that automatic perception isn't always useful.

6. Make realistic objectives

Consider defining short goals as an alternative to creating a big list of chores. A sense of control, success, and drive may be gained through setting and achieving these goals.

Achievable objectives could be:

• Take out the garbage instead of cleaning the house.

• Sort the piles of clothes so you don't have to do them all at once.

• Only respond to time-sensitive emails rather than emptying your whole inbox.

Focus on another tiny task after completing the first one, then another. In this manner, rather of an unfinished to-do list, you have a list of concrete accomplishments.

7. Recognize your work.

All objectives are deserving of honor, and all accomplishments are cause for celebration. Try your best to acknowledge when you reach a goal.

Recognizing your own achievements may be a potent strategy for combating the negative effects of depression, even if you don't feel like having a cake and throwing confetti because of them.

It may be especially effective to resist negative self-talk and over generalization with memories of a task well done.

8. Establish a routine

A flexible schedule may provide you a sense of control if your everyday activities are disrupted by depression symptoms. These schedules don't have to cover the whole day.

Create a flexible schedule with some structure to help you maintain your daily pace.

9. Engage in enjoyable behavior

You can feel so exhausted that you give up. In comparison to desired feelings, it could feel stronger.

Try to fight back by doing something you enjoy or that is importance for you. It may be singing, dancing, drawing, motorcycling, or playing an instrument.

By improving your mood or energy via meaningful activity, you may be further inspired to carry on with activities that assist in coping with symptoms.

10. Take in some music

According to research, listening to music can help with depression symptoms and mood. Additionally, it could make it easier for you to feel warm emotions.

When music is played in groups, like a band or musical ensemble, it can be very useful. The same benefits may also be obtained by merely listening.

11. Take in the outdoors

A person's mood may be greatly influenced by spending time in nature. Nature walks, according to research, may help those who suffer from severe depression feel better about themselves.

Spending time outdoors may enhance mood and cognition while reducing the risk of mental health issues.

However, the direct impact of nature on those with clinical depression has received relatively little investigation.

Take a stroll through the woods at lunchtime or spend some time at your neighborhood park. Or schedule a weekend trek. While getting some sun, these activities might help you re-connect with nature.

12. Invest time in your loved ones.

Face-to-face interaction might help wash away these impulses. Depression can entice you to retreat from the people you love and trust.

Calls or video chats might be useful if you can't physically spend time together.

Try to keep in mind that these folks genuinely care about you. Don't give in to the urge to feel like a burden. Both of you probably need the interaction.

13. Let your emotions be known

Think considering keeping a journal or writing about your feelings. When the emotions subside, write about that as well. According to Research, journalism can be a helpful adjunct treatment for managing mental health issues.

It might be easier to convey how you're feeling when you write your ideas down. Additionally, it can assist you in tracking your everyday symptoms and determining their root causes.

You might resolve to write for a little while every day or week. Most importantly, it's entirely up to you what you want to write about.

14. Do something completely different

You employ the same brain regions while performing the same task repeatedly.

In addition to potentially enhancing your general well-being and fortifying your social connections, trying new activities may be gratifying.

Consider taking up a new activity, artistic endeavor, or cooking skill to enjoy these advantages.

15. Consider volunteering.

By volunteering and donating your time to someone or something else, you may kill two birds with one stone—spending time with others and learning something new.

Even though you might be accustomed to getting assistance from pals, your mental health might be enhanced more by reaching out and offering assistance.

Bonus: Volunteering has positive effects on a person's physical health. Among them include a decreased risk of hypertension and enhanced sleep.

16. Show gratitude

By giving thanks for what you have, whether it be a favorite hobby or something new, you might be able to improve your mental health.

Gratitude exercises might have enduring benefits for your general mental health.

Additionally, it may be particularly significant to express your thankfulness in writing, including in messages to other people.

17. Practice meditation.

Depression symptoms can be prolonged by stress and worry. You may reduce your stress and bring more joy and harmony into your day by learning relaxing methods. According to research from a reliable source, practicing mindfulness may enhance your sense of well-being and make you feel more aware of your surroundings.

These can be the following:

• contemplation

• yoga

• deep inhaling

• Journaling

18. Eat healthily

There isn't a miracle diet that can cure depression. But how you feel may actually and significantly be impacted by what you consume in your body.

When they stay away from processed meals, sugar, and preservatives, some individuals report feeling better and having more energy.

If you can, think about consulting a qualified nutritionist or doctor for advice.

A good place to start could be eating a diet high in lean meats, veggies, and grains. Limit your consumption of depressants like alcohol and stimulants like caffeine in coffee, soda, and tea.

19. Think about reducing your alcohol and drug use.

substances, such as alcohol or narcotics may help keep negative emotions alive.

On the other side, those who struggle with addiction may exhibit depressive symptoms.

If you wish to relieve your depression symptoms, you might want to reduce or stop using alcohol and other drugs.

20. Maintain good sleep habits

Sleep issues are typical of depression. You can have trouble sleeping or sleep too much. Both can exacerbate the symptoms of depression.

Sleep for a minimum of 8 hours each night. Try to establish a regular sleeping schedule.

It might be beneficial to go to bed and wake up at the same time each day if you want to keep to a routine. You could feel more balanced and energized during the day if you get enough sleep.

21. Recognize the truth in your feelings

It could seem like a wise move to organize and suppress your emotions in order to deal with the challenging depression symptoms. However, this method is ultimately harmful and unsuccessful.

Recognize if you're having a bad day. Try to direct your attention away from your emotions and toward engaging in things that are beneficial rather than dwelling on them. Notice and label your emotions.

Understanding how depression symptoms come and go can be helpful for self-healing and clinging to hope.

CHAPTER ONE

UNDERSTANDING DEPRESSION

Millions of people worldwide are affected by the common and complicated mental health disorder known as depression. Depression is much more than a passing sensation, despite the fact that it's frequently used as a catch-all phrase for feeling depressed. It is a significant condition that is frequently persistent and has an impact on a person's emotions, thoughts, and actions. Relationships can suffer, it can be very difficult to work and stay healthy, and in extreme circumstances, it might even result in suicide. Adults, teenagers, and children are all susceptible. It is distinct from the mood swings that people often encounter on a daily basis.

To effectively combat depression, it's crucial to gain a deep understanding of its nature and how it manifests.

1. Profound Sadness and Emptiness: A persistent and pervasive feeling of sadness, emptiness, or hopelessness is a hallmark of depression. This emotional state tends to last throughout the day almost every day and is not in line with the conditions of life.

2. Loss of Interest and Pleasure: People who are depressed frequently lose interest in or pleasure from past interests. Anhedonia is a disorder that can make it difficult to do simple self-care duties.

3. Physical and cognitive symptoms: Physical signs of depression include changes in food and weight, insomnia or hypersomnia, exhaustion, and problems focusing, making decisions, or recalling information.

4. A negative view of oneself: Many depressed persons have emotions of worthlessness, excessive guilt, or self-criticism. They frequently talk negatively to themselves because they feel they are a burden to others or have failed in some manner.

5. Social Withdrawal: People who are depressed may stop participating in social activities, which can cause isolation and strained relationships. This withdrawal may both originate from and contribute to the continuation of depression.

6. Physical Symptoms: People who are depressed can get physical symptoms including headaches, gastrointestinal issues, or inexplicable aches and pains.

The Complexity of Depression

There is no one treatment for depression. Each person will experience it differently, and the severity might vary. While some people may have persistent depression, others may just have sporadic depressed episodes. Furthermore, it can be difficult to diagnose and successfully treat depression when it coexists with other mental health illnesses like anxiety or drug use disorders.

Depression in women

Researchers do not know why depression appears to be more frequent in girls when it is nearly twice as common in boys. A 2021 research, however, suggests that the discrepancy could be caused by inconsistent reporting. Researchers discovered that women were more likely than men to report having depressive symptoms and to seek therapy.

According to certain studies, being subjected to gender discrimination raises the likelihood of developing depression.

Additionally, some forms of depression, such as postpartum depression and premenstrual dysphoric disorder, are exclusive to women.

Depression in men

Men with depression are more prone than women to consume excessive amounts of alcohol, act out in anger, and take risks.

Among the other signs of depression in men are:

Shunning social and family gatherings; working nonstop; struggling to balance job and family obligations; and exhibiting harsh or domineering conduct in relationships.

Depression in College students

A person may be coping with different lives, cultures, and experiences for the first time throughout their time at college, which can be difficult.

Some students struggle to adjust to these changes, and as a result, they may experience despair, anxiety, or both.

College students who are depressed may struggle to focus on their studies, experience sleeplessness, sleep excessively, experience changes in their appetite, avoid social situations and activities they formerly enjoyed, and exhibit other symptoms as well.

Depression in Adolescent years

Teenage depression can be brought on by physical changes, peer pressure, and other circumstances.

They could suffer a few of the symptoms listed below:

• Irritability;

• Restlessness, such as the difficulty to remain seated

• Retreating from family and friends

• Trouble focusing on academics

• A sense of remorse, helplessness, or worthlessness

Depression in Children

Children who are depressed may find it difficult to engage in academic and social activities. They may display signs like sobbing, poor energy, clinginess, rebellious conduct, and loud outbursts.

Younger children can find it challenging to verbally communicate their emotions. They may find it more difficult to communicate their unhappiness as a result.

Understanding depression's complexity, the range of symptoms it exhibits, and the multiple elements that influence its development is essential to comprehend it. Individuals, families, and society as a whole may strive toward more effectively identifying, treating, and ultimately conquering this difficult mental health disease by having a thorough understanding of depression. It is a journey that starts with awareness and empathetic understanding and progresses toward successful intervention and support.

Importance of Addressing Depression

There can be little doubt that depression is a major public health issue on a worldwide scale. Beyond only the person who experiences it, it has an influence on families, communities, businesses, and society as a whole. Dealing with depression is crucial for a number of important reasons:

1. Personal Well-Being: Depression severely reduces a person's quality of life. It deprives them of the capacity to feel joy, engage in worthwhile pursuits, and preserve good relationships. By treating depression, we put the well-being of people who are affected first and work to help them regain the capacity to live happy lives.

2. Physical Health: Depression affects more than just mental health; it can also have physical effects. It can cause changes in appetite, sleep problems, chronic pain, and a higher chance of contracting other illnesses including diabetes and heart disease. Treatment for depression can lead to better physical health results.

3. Suicide prevention: Depression is a major contributing factor to suicide globally. If untreated, it can worsen to the point that a person considers or makes an attempt at suicide. The risk of suicide can be considerably reduced and lives can be saved with prompt intervention and therapy.

4. Economic Repercussions: Depression has significant economic repercussions. It causes absenteeism, poor business productivity, and higher healthcare expenditures. In addition to helping individual employees, addressing melancholy in the workplace promotes a more efficient and cost-effective company.

5. Reducing Stigma: Dealing with depression helps to lessen the stigma attached to mental health problems. When we openly talk about and support individuals who suffer from depression, we build a more accepting and understanding culture that inspires others to get assistance without worrying about being judged.

6. Preventing Long-Term Effects: If depression is not treated, it can develop into a chronic condition that results in recurrent bouts and even lifetime difficulties. Early intervention can stop the emergence of persistent depression and its accompanying problems.

7. Family and Social Relationships: Depression may cause tension in friendships and family ties, which can result in social disengagement and isolation. By addressing depression, these vital social ties can be strengthened and rebuilt.

8. Increasing Resilience: An important component of effective depression therapy is educating patients on how to deal with stress and adversity. This component of developing resilience is important for overcoming depression as well as confronting obstacles in the future.

9. Fostering a Healthier Society: A society that tackles mental health and depressive disorders generates higher levels of general well-being. When mental health is given priority, we build a more caring and sympathetic society where people feel respected and supported.

10. Global Impact: Depression is a problem that affects everyone. We can support worldwide initiatives to enhance mental health and lessen the burden of sickness by treating it.

It is not only important for one's own health but also for society as a whole to address depression. It has wide-ranging effects on people and their families, as well as on their jobs and communities. We can significantly improve the lives of individuals afflicted by depression and promote a healthier, more compassionate society by emphasizing mental health, decreasing stigma, and providing access to effective therapies and support networks.

CHAPTER TWO

TYPES OF DEPRESSION

A. Major Depressive Disorder (MDD)

Major Depressive Disorder (MDD), also referred to as depression, is a common and incarcerating mental health disorder characterized by intense and persistent feelings of sorrow, despair, and a lack of interest or enjoyment in most activities. It is one of the most prevalent mental health conditions worldwide and may significantly affect a person's life.

Key Characteristics of Major Depressive Disorder

1. Persistent Low Mood: For at least two weeks, a persistently low mood that lasts for the majority of the day, almost every day, is the primary sign of MDD. This feeling is frequently characterized as intense melancholy, emptiness, or hopelessness.

2. Anhedonia: Anhedonia is the lessened capacity for enjoyment or interest in once-pleasant activities. People who have MDD frequently lose interest in their passions, relationships, and even routine self-care.

3. Physical and cognitive symptoms: Physical signs of depression include changes in food and weight, insomnia or hypersomnia, exhaustion, and problems focusing, making decisions, or recalling information.

4. Thoughts of Worthlessness or Guilt: A lot of people with MDD struggle with strong emotions of inadequacy, excessive guilt, or self-criticism. It's possible that they feel they are a burden or that they have failed in some way.

5. Psychomotor Alterations: Depression can affect how a person moves. Others may have psychomotor retardation, which results in sluggish motions and speech, while other people may experience psychomotor agitation, which makes them restless and fidgety.

6. Suicidal Thoughts: People with MDD may experience suicidal or death thoughts in extreme circumstances. Suicidal thoughts is always severe and need to be treated right away by a specialist.

Major depressive Disorder is a serious mental illness marked by severe and persistent depressed symptoms. To offer the essential support and resources for those afflicted by MDD and to lessen the stigma associated with mental health difficulties, it is imperative for individuals, families, and society at large to have a thorough understanding of its symptoms, causes, and available therapies.

Many people with MDD can substantially alleviate their symptoms and move on to lead full lives with the right support and therapy. It's crucial to keep in mind that rehabilitation could be a slow process and that relapses might happen. Long-term well-being requires continuing self-care and regular follow-up with mental health experts.

B. Dysthymia, or persistent depressive disorder

A persistent and frequently misunderstood mood disease is persistent depressive disorder (PDD), originally known as dysthymia. PDD contains long-lasting, less severe symptoms of depression that endure for at least two years or more in adults and one year or more in adolescents and children. This is in contrast to Major Depressive Disorder (MDD), which is characterized by severe but episodic depressive episodes.

The main characteristics of persistent depressive disorders are:

1. Chronic Low Mood: A chronically low mood that lasts for an extended period of time is the main feature of PDD. PDD is frequently described by those who experience it as a pervasive melancholy, despair, or "just not feeling right." Nearly every day, these emotions last the majority of the day.

2. Additional Depressive Symptoms: Other depressed symptoms, such as changes in eating or weight, sleep issues, exhaustion, poor self-esteem, trouble focusing, and hopelessness, may accompany chronic low mood in people with PDD.

3. Less Severe than MDD: While the symptoms of PDD are widespread and persistent, they are often less than those of Major Depressive Disorder. However, the chronic nature of the condition has the potential to seriously impact everyday living and overall quality of life.

4. Coexistence with Other Mental Health diseases: People with PDD may also have Major Depressive Disorder episodes, sometimes known as "double depression," or they may have comorbid diseases including anxiety disorders or drug use disorders.

Even though persistent depressive disorder is a chronic disease, it is manageable with the correct mix of therapies and assistance. The aim is to enhance the person's capacity to function despite persistent low mood, not necessarily to completely resolve all symptoms. For long-term well-being, regular follow-up with mental health specialists is crucial.

In conclusion, Dysthymia, also known as Persistent depression illness, is a long-term mood illness marked by a persistently low mood and extra depression symptoms. The first stages in managing this illness and raising the quality of life for PDD sufferers are recognizing the signs and symptoms, getting the right care, and offering continuing support.

C. Bipolar Disorder

Millions of individuals worldwide are afflicted by bipolar disorder, a complicated and sometimes misunderstood mental illness. Extreme mood and energy swings are its hallmarks, which can make it difficult for sufferers to adequately manage their everyday lives. Periods of mania or hypomania (high mood) and depression (low mood) are distinctive features of this condition.

Major life changes, trauma, and stressful life events can start or aggravate bipolar episodes.

Types of Bipolar Disorder

There are various subtypes of bipolar disorder, with Bipolar I and II being the most prevalent:

1. Bipolar I Disorder: People with Bipolar I disorder go through full-blown manic episodes, which are defined by periods of heightened, irritated, or ecstatic mood that last at least one week and frequently involve symptoms that make it difficult to go about everyday tasks. There are also depressive episodes.

2. Bipolar II Disorder: This condition is characterized by an alternation of hypomanic (less severe) episodes and depressed episodes. The symptoms of hypomania are milder than those of complete mania and last for a shorter time.

3. Cyclothymic Disorder: This subtype is characterized by recurrent episodes of hypomania and depression that last at least two years (one year in kids and teenagers).

Features of Bipolar Disorder

1. Mania or Hypomania: During manic or hypomanic episodes, people may feel more energized, their thoughts may race, they may need less sleep, they may have an inflated sense of self-worth, they may be impulsive, and they may engage in risky activities.

2. Depression: Depressive episodes are characterized by feelings of melancholy, despair, lack of interest or enjoyment in the majority of activities, exhaustion, changes in eating or weight, disturbed sleep, and trouble focusing.

3. Cycling: The fluctuation between these extremes is a hallmark of bipolar illness. Individual differences in episode frequency and length are significant.

The dramatic mood swings between mania or hypomania and depression are the hallmarks of bipolar illness. Although it can be difficult to manage, bipolar disorder sufferers can successfully control their symptoms and lead fulfilling lives with early diagnosis and thorough treatment.

Bipolar disease sufferers can enjoy happy lives with the right care and assistance. Long-term stability requires frequent counseling, medication compliance, and lifestyle control. It's crucial to remember that each person's experience with bipolar illness is unique and that continuous treatment is frequently required.

D. Seasonal Affective Disorder (SAD)

The impact of seasonal changes on mental health, occasionally referred to as "winter depression" or "seasonal depression,". Seasonal Affective Disorder

(SAD) is a form of depression that has a seasonal rhythm. It is characterized by recurrent depressive episodes, which usually happen in the fall and winter when there is less sunshine. SAD is a widely known mental health syndrome that mostly affects persons in areas with severe seasonal fluctuations.

Although the exact etiology of Seasonal Affective Disorder is unknown, several variables may play a role in its emergence:

- Since less sunshine throughout the winter months can influence these natural cycles, disruptions in the body's internal biological clock and circadian rhythms may contribute to SAD.

- Serotonin and melatonin are neurotransmitters that control mood and sleep, and variations in sunshine exposure can affect their synthesis.

☐ Since SAD frequently runs in families, there may be a hereditary susceptibility to developing it.

☐ SAD is more prevalent in areas with significant seasonal daylight fluctuations, such as in higher latitudes where the winters are darker and longer.

Important Characteristics of Seasonal Affective Disorder:

1. Seasonal Pattern: SAD symptoms often start in the late fall or early winter and go away in the spring or summer. A less prevalent variant termed "summer SAD" affects certain people, and symptoms appear throughout the summer.

2. Depressive Symptoms: Many of the symptoms of serious depression, such as chronic sorrow, despair, and a loss of interest or enjoyment in activities, are also present in SAD. Changes in appetite and weight, sleep issues, exhaustion, trouble focusing, and social disengagement are among the other typical symptoms.

3. Hypersensitivity to Light: Some people with SAD may have a hypersensitivity to light, which makes them want for more sunshine and makes them feel better when they are in bright light.

4. Social and Occupational Impairment: SAD can affect social interactions and work performance since the symptoms might make it difficult to go about everyday tasks.

Most people with SAD may resume their regular activities during the appropriate seasons and find considerable symptom improvement with the right therapy and self-care techniques. It's critical for people with SAD to notice the beginning of symptoms, get the support they need, and take proactive measures to control their disease.

E. Postpartum Depression: Navigating the Challenges of Motherhood

Postpartum depression (PPD), sometimes known as postnatal depression and affecting some women and, in rare instances, males after giving birth to a child, is a frequent and complicated mental health issue. Understanding the particular difficulties and experiences related to PPD is critical since prompt identification and assistance are essential for the well-being of both the parent and the child.

The precise underlying biological, psychological, and environmental causes of PPD are complex and interrelated:

- **Hormonal Changes:** It is thought that PPD is influenced by abrupt changes in hormone levels, notably a sharp decline in estrogen and progesterone following delivery.

- **Biological Vulnerability:** PPD risk is increased in those with a history of mood disorders including depression or bipolar disorder.

- **Psychological Factors:** PPD risk can be increased by stress, a history of trauma or abuse, a lack of social support, and perfectionist tendencies.

- **Lack of Sleep:** Taking care of a baby might cause sleep problems that can make depression symptoms worse.

- Transition to Parenthood: The additional obligations and lifestyle adjustments that come with being a parent might make it difficult to adjust.

Features of PPD

1. Timing: PPD often manifests itself in the initial weeks to months following childbirth. Any kid can give birth to it, whether it is the first or later one, or even a loss or miscarriage.

2. Depressive Symptoms: Many of the symptoms of severe depression, such as chronic melancholy, despair, and a lack of enthusiasm or enjoyment in activities, are also present in PPD. Changes in appetite and weight, sleep issues, exhaustion, irritability, anxiety, and difficulties focusing are some more typical symptoms.

3. Mother-Infant Bond: PPD can impair a mother's capacity to care for and bond with her infant, which can result in feelings of guilt and parental inadequacy.

4. Social and Professional Impact: PPD can interfere with daily activities, such as relationships and professional obligations, adding further stress to the new parents.

F. Atypical Depression

Atypical Depression is a sub-type of major depressive disorder (MDD) distinguished from typical depression by a unique set of symptoms. Atypical depression can include mood swings, an increase in hunger, excessive sleeping, and a heavy feeling in the limbs. Although difficult to identify, this type of depression must be understood in order to receive the proper care.

Key features of Atypical Depression

1. Mood Reactivity: Mood reactivity is one of the distinguishing characteristics of atypical depression. This implies that even though their mood is generally down, people with this illness might feel happier in reaction to happy occasions or news.

2. Increased hunger: People with atypical depression frequently report increased hunger and desires, particularly for carbohydrate-rich meals, in contrast to people with normal depression, when appetite frequently declines.

3. Hypersomnia: Atypical depression is linked to excessive daytime drowsiness or prolonged sleep, which is frequently characterized by afternoon naps, extended overnight sleep, and trouble getting up in the morning.

4. Leaden Paralysis: Some sufferers with atypical depression report feeling heavy or paralyzed in their limbs, which can be upsetting and add to weariness.

5. Sensitivity to Rejection: People with atypical depression may be particularly sensitive to social rejection as perceived, which can cause interpersonal issues and raise the chance of social withdrawal.

6. Additional Depressive Symptoms: In addition to these unique traits, people with this subtype might also have regular sorrow, poor energy, feelings of worthlessness, and trouble focusing.

CHAPTER THREE

CAUSES OF DEPRESSION

The complex and multidimensional mental health disease of depression is impacted by a number of risk factors and causes. For both prevention and efficient treatment, it is crucial to comprehend these fundamental causes.

The Major Causes of Depression

❖ Biological Factors

Understanding the Neurochemical and Genetic Complexity

A major contributing component in the emergence of depression is biological. These elements, which include complex brain-body connections, help us understand why certain people are more susceptible to this mental health issue. Further detail on the biochemical causes of depression:

1. Imbalances in neurotransmitters:

Serotonin is a neurotransmitter that is frequently linked to mood modulation. Low serotonin levels have been related to depressive symptoms such as irritability and protracted melancholy.

• **Norepinephrine:** This neurotransmitter has an impact on arousal and alertness. Norepinephrine levels that are out of whack might cause symptoms including exhaustion, sleep disruptions, and attention problems.

• **Dopamine:** Although dopamine is frequently linked to rewards and pleasure, dopamine imbalances can lead to anhedonia, a major depressive symptom marked by a decreased capacity for enjoyment.

• **Glutamate:** An excitatory neurotransmitter involved in memory and learning. Depression symptoms are linked to abnormalities in glutamate activity.

2. Genetic Predisposition:

• **Family History:** With a history of depression in one's family might greatly raise one's risk. About 40–50% of the chance of having depression is influenced by genetics.

• **Candidate Genes:** Research has pinpointed several genes that may be related to a person's propensity for depression. These genes frequently have connections to brain flexibility and neurotransmitter modulation.

3. Brain Organization and Activity:

• **Hippocampus:** People with depression frequently have a smaller Hippocampus, a part of the brain that controls memory and emotions. Hippocampal atrophy may be exacerbated by ongoing stress and high cortisol levels.

• **Prefrontal Cortex:** The prefrontal cortex, which is involved in decision-making, problem-solving, and emotional control, may have altered activity and connection in depressed individuals.

• **Amygdala:** People with depression may exhibit increased activity and sensitivity in the amygdala, which is involved in processing emotions, in reaction to unfavorable stimuli.

4. Hormonal Influences:

• **Endocrine System:** When the secretion of hormones is misregulated, they can affect mood and cause depression, especially cortisol (the stress hormone).

• **Thyroid hormones:** Depressive symptoms may be brought on by thyroid dysfunction, which is defined by abnormal thyroid hormone levels. Low thyroid function, or hypothyroidism, is linked to the frequent depressive symptoms of exhaustion and low energy.

5. Inflammatory Processes:

• **Chronic inflammation** in the body, which may be related to immune system dysregulation, may have a role in the emergence of depression, according to a recent study.

6. Neuroplasticity:

• **Neurogenesis:** Depression affects the brain's capacity to produce new neurons (neurogenesis) and create new neural connections (neuroplasticity). Reduced neuroplasticity may make it more difficult for the brain to adjust to stress.

It is essential to comprehend the biological causes of depression in order to develop effective treatment plans. Neurotransmitter imbalances are intended to be fixed by medications like selective serotonin reuptake inhibitors (SSRIs) and other antidepressants. Additionally, depression symptoms are reduced and brain connections are reshaped using neuroplasticity-targeting therapies including cognitive-behavioral therapy (CBT) and mindfulness-based interventions.

❖ Environmental Factors in Depression

Unraveling the Impact of the External World

Depression is not entirely caused by internal issues; environmental elements from the outside world also have a big impact on how it develops. These environmental variables include a broad spectrum of situations and life events that may be responsible for the development or escalation of depression symptoms.

1. Life Events and Stressors:

• **Major Life Changes:** Depressive episodes can be brought on by significant life changes including the death of a loved one, divorce, losing a job, or relocating. These occurrences cause emotional upheaval and disruption of regular routines.

• **Chronic Stress:** Prolonged exposure to chronic stress, frequently brought on by obligations in the areas of job, economics, or caring, might aid in the emergence of depression.

• **Trauma:** Being exposed to traumatic situations like physical or sexual abuse increases the likelihood of getting depression. In these circumstances, depression frequently coexists with post-traumatic stress disorder (PTSD).

2. Childhood Adversity

• **Early-Life Adversity:** Negative early experiences, such as abuse, neglect, or dysfunctional families, can have a lifelong impact on mental health. People who were maltreated or subjected to trauma as children may be more prone to depression as adults.

3. Socioeconomic Factors

• **Economic Hardship:** Uncertainty about one's future, unemployment, and poverty can lead to ongoing stress and restrict access to services that support mental health, making depression more likely.

• **work and Education:** Lack of work and educational possibilities can exacerbate emotions of inadequacy and pessimism, which are elements frequently linked to depression.

4. Social Support and Relationships

• **Social Isolation:** Studies show that greater rates of depression are linked to social isolation and emotions of loneliness. Strong social networks and dependable connections can function as inhibitors of the onset of depression.

• **Interpersonal Disagreements:** Constant disagreements, strained relationships, or social rejection can raise stress and aggravate depression symptoms.

• **Cultural Expectations:** Cultural norms and expectations surrounding gender roles, achievement, and emotional expression might affect a person's vulnerability to depression.

• **Stigma:** People who suffer from mental illness may be reluctant to seek assistance, which can result in delayed or ineffective treatment.

5. Seasonal and Environmental Factors

• **Seasonal Affective Disorder (SAD):** Variations in natural light throughout the year can affect mood and exacerbate depression symptoms, especially in areas with lengthy, gloomy winters.

• **Pollution and Toxins:** Though study in this area is continuing, exposure to environmental pollutants and toxins has been investigated as a potential risk factor for depression.

For preventative and therapeutic efforts to be successful, it is essential to comprehend the environmental elements linked to depression. The risk and effects of depression can be reduced by recognizing and dealing with these outside stressors, fostering resilience, and encouraging social support networks. Additionally, because treating both internal and external influences is essential to successful care, healthcare practitioners take these aspects into account when designing treatment programs for those who are depressed.

❖ Psychological Factors in Depression: The Mind-Body Connection.

An important part of the development and presentation of depression is also played by psychological variables. The psychological components of this mental health issue include a person's ideas, feelings, beliefs, and coping techniques, adding to its complexity.

1. Negative mental habits

• **Cognitive Triad:** Aaron Beck's idea of the cognitive triad describes negative beliefs about one's self, the outside world, and the future. People who suffer from depression frequently hold skewed and gloomy ideas in these domains, which adds to feelings of hopelessness and unworthiness.

• **Rumination:** Rehashing unpleasant memories and ideas continually in one's head is known as persistent rumination. Rumination like this might lengthen and exacerbate depression episodes.

2. Self-Worth and Self-Esteem

• **Poor self-esteem:** Depression is frequently linked to poor self-esteem and a negative self-concept. People may believe they are undeserving of pleasure, unlovable, or insufficient.

3. Coping Techniques

• **Maladaptive Coping:** Depressive symptoms can be made worse by unhealthy coping strategies such as avoidance, substance abuse, or emotional repression. Although they could offer short-term solace, these tactics exacerbate long-term pain.

• **Coping Deficits:** People who struggle to cope with stresses may lack the capacity to solve problems or control their emotions, which makes them more susceptible to depression.

4. Personality traits

• **Neuroticism**, which is characterized by emotional instability and negative emotionality and is linked to a higher risk of depression.

• **Perfectionism:** Excessive perfectionism and unreasonable expectations can result in ongoing self-criticism and failure-related sentiments, which can worsen depression symptoms.

5. Interpersonal Relationships

• **Attachment Styles:** Early experiences with attachment can change a person's patterns of relationships, which can affect their susceptibility to depression. The risk may be increased by insecure attachment patterns like nervous or avoidant behavior.

Interpersonal conflicts can exacerbate depressive symptoms by causing feelings of loneliness and melancholy. These interactions might be with friends, family, or romantic partners.

6. Stress and Coping with Life Events

• **Stressful Life Events:** How people react to and handle life's stresses might have an impact on how depressed they become. Vulnerability may be worsened by inadequate coping mechanisms or a lack of adaptive coping techniques.

7. Personality Disorders

Borderline Personality Disorder (BPD): People with BPD are more likely to suffer mood fluctuations and may have severe, episodic depression symptoms.

It is essential to comprehend the psychological causes of depression in order to avoid and treat it. For instance, cognitive-behavioral therapy (CBT) focuses on unhelpful thought patterns and assists people in creating better coping skills. Similarly to this, interpersonal therapy (IPT) emphasizes enhancing relationships with others, which helps lessen symptoms of depression. These treatment methods seek to address the psychological aspects of depression by providing people with tools to more effectively control their emotions, thought, and behavior

❖ Emotional Symptoms of Depression: Understanding the Internal Unrest

An individual's well-being is frequently impacted by the complex interplay of emotional symptoms that characterize depression and are essential to its diagnosis. The severe emotional discomfort and dysregulation that go along with this mental health disorder are reflected in these emotional symptoms.

The emotional aspects of depression are as follows:

1. Constant Sadness

Deep and Widespread: An intense and enduring sensation of melancholy or a low mood that lasts for most of the day, almost every day, is one of the defining signs of depression.

2. Hopelessness

Loss of Optimism: People who are depressed frequently feel completely hopeless about the future. They could think that nothing would ever change, which would make them depressed.

3. Emptiness

Feeling Numb: Some people who are depressed talk about feeling emotionally empty or numb. Even in circumstances that would ordinarily generate joyful or enthusiastic responses, they could find it difficult to feel these feelings.

4. Anhedonia

Lack of Interest in Previously Pleasurable Activities: Anhedonia is the inability to feel pleasure or interest in previously pleasurable activities. Loss of interest in hobbies, social activities, or even close relationships might result from this emotional ailment.

5. Irritation

Increased Sensitivity: Although depression is frequently linked to melancholy, it can also show itself as irritation. Even in reaction to mild pressures, people can quickly become irritated, upset, or angry.

6. Guilt and Worthlessness

People with depression frequently suffer tremendous guilt and feelings of worthlessness.

Excessive Self-Criticism. They could feel responsible for their illness or like a burden to others.

7. Anxiety

Co-Occurrence: Depression and anxiety symptoms usually co-occur. Along with their melancholy feelings, people may also suffer excessive concern, agitation, and a sense of approaching doom.

8. Suicidal Thoughts

Desire to Escape: Severe depression can result in thoughts of suicide or self-harm. Some people may believe that the only way to get rid of their emotional suffering is by taking their own life.

9. Emotional Lability

Rapid Mood Swings: People who are having depressive episodes may exhibit emotional instability, changing their moods quickly between sorrow, rage, and other emotions.

10. Emotional tiredness

Overwhelming Fatigue: Depression's emotional toll can cause extreme tiredness. People may experience emotional exhaustion and lack of energy for normal everyday tasks.

It is crucial for both diagnosis and treatment that these emotional symptoms are recognized and understood.

❖ Cognitive Symptoms of Depression: mental fog of despair

Depression has a significant impact on cognitive performance in addition to its emotional side effects. These cognitive symptoms may be upsetting and incapacitating, impairing a person's capacity for clear thought, concentration, decision-making, and day-to-day functioning.

Their features include:

1. Lack of Focus and Concentration

Mental Fog: Depression frequently results in a feeling of cognitive confusion. People could have trouble maintaining their concentration, paying attention to tasks, or remembering information.

2. Memory Issues

Forgetting Things: Depressive symptoms can cause issues with functioning and short-term memory, which can result in forgetfulness and absentmindedness.

3. Indecisiveness

Difficulty Making Decisions: People with depression may find it difficult to make even straightforward decisions because they may obsess over their alternatives or worry that they will make the incorrect choice.

4. Negative Cognitive Bias

Selective Attention: Depression frequently results in a negative bias in thinking, where people give greater weight to and focus on unfavorable information or events while ignoring favorable ones.

5. Excessive Self-Criticism and Negative Self-Talk

Internal Critic: People who are depressed may engage in excessive self-criticism and negative self-talk, which serves to reinforce feelings of worthlessness.

6. Slowed Thinking

Depression can decrease cognitive processing speed, making it challenging to engage in tasks that call for fast thinking or problem-solving.

Reduced Processing Speed: Depression can impair cerebral processing speed.

7. Rumination

Rumination is a distinctive psychological symptom of depression and is characterized by recurrent, bothersome thoughts about regrets, errors, or unpleasant events.

8. Lack of Mental Clarity

Difficulty Thinking Clearly: Many depressed people report experiencing overall cognitive fuzziness or mental tiredness, which impairs their capacity for clear, logical thought.

9. Perceptual Changes

Warped Perception of Time: Some depressed people claim that time feels deformed, with days passing unusually slowly or rapidly.

Distorted Perception of Time: People who are depressed can feel as though time is moving at an inconsistent pace, with the days passing slowly or fast.

10. Lessened Creativity

Depression may hinder creative thinking and problem-solving skills, which makes it harder to come up with original ideas or solutions.

These cognitive symptoms can considerably affect a person's performance in a variety of spheres of life, including employment, relationships, and self-care, in addition to being stressful. Effective depression care depends on identifying and treating these cognitive symptoms. People can restore cognitive clarity, strengthen decision-making skills, and improve general cognitive functioning with the use of treatment alternatives including cognitive-behavioral therapy (CBT).

❖ Physical symptoms of depression: when the body bears the weight of the mind

Depression also has a significant influence on the body, manifesting as physical symptoms when the body carries the weight of the mind. These physical signs and symptoms, which frequently resemble other medical disorders, can be crippling. For a thorough diagnosis and course of therapy, it is crucial to comprehend and recognize these bodily signs of depression.

Let's look at the physical aspects of depression.

1. Low energy and fatigue

• Consistent fatigue Even after a full night's sleep, people with depression frequently feel extremely lethargic and lack energy. It might be difficult to carry out everyday tasks because of this exhaustion, which can be paralyzing.

2. Sleep Disorders

• Insomnia: A typical sign of sadness is difficulty sleeping or staying asleep. Insufficient sleep can make tiredness and depressive symptoms worse.

• Hypersomnia: In certain situations, depression can result in excessive sleep or sleepiness that lasts for lengthy stretches of time, even throughout the day.

3. Appetite and Weight Changes

• Changes in hunger: Depression may have a variety of effects on hunger. Some people could have a significant decrease in appetite, which would result in weight reduction, whilst other people would overeat and put on weight.

• Cravings: Depressive episodes can be accompanied by particular eating cravings, frequently for comfort or high-carb meals.

4. Pains & Aches

• Physical Discomfort: Headaches, joint pain, and muscle aches are among the undiagnosed aches and pains that frequently accompany depression.

5. Gastrointestinal Symptoms

• Digestive Problems: Depression can make symptoms like stomachaches, indigestion, and irritable bowel syndrome (IBS) worse.

6. Psychomotor Symptoms

• Sluggishness: Psychomotor retardation, which causes sluggish movements, speech, and responses, can be a symptom of depression.

• Agitation: People with depression may exhibit psychomotor agitation, which is characterized by restlessness and the difficulty of sitting motionless.

7. Decreased Libido

• Sexual Dysfunction: Depression can cause a decrease in sex-related interest and desire as well as problems obtaining or keeping an erection or arousal.

8. Changes in Appearance:

• Ignoring Personal Care: Depressed people may ignore their grooming and hygiene practices, which can leave them looking noticeably worse off.

9. Weakened immune function

• Increased Vulnerability: Long-term anxiety and depression can compromise immunological function, leaving people more prone to infections and diseases.

10. Cardiovascular Health

• Higher Risk: Depression is linked to an increased risk of heart attacks and strokes, probably as a result of the effects of chronic stress on the cardiovascular system.

These physical signs of depression frequently coincide with emotional and cognitive signs, adding to the condition's total burden. It's critical to understand that these physical symptoms are a component of the larger depression illness and not just the outcome of a "mind over matter" strategy. It is essential to seek professional assistance and the proper care, which may include psychotherapy, medication, lifestyle modifications, and self-care techniques, in order to address the mental and physical elements of depression and enhance general well-being.

❖ **Behavior-Based Depression Symptoms: Outward Expressions of Internal Unrest**

A person's conduct may also be a sign of depression. These behavioral symptoms can have a big influence on everyday living, relationships, and general quality of life. They are frequently obvious to others.

We explore the behavioral aspects of depression as follows:

1. Social Exclusion

• Isolation: Due to emotions of despair, guilt, or a lack of interest in social connections, people with depression may avoid friends and family, withdraw from social activities, and isolate themselves.

2. Decreased Productivity

• Work and Academic Performance: Depression can cause a loss in productivity, which can lead to missed workdays, poor job performance, and problems in academic settings.

• Procrastination: Depressed people may find it difficult to start projects or finish assignments, frequently pushing off their obligations.

3. Neglect of Responsibilities

• Household chores: People with depression frequently struggle to keep up with everyday obligations like housecleaning, bill paying, or running errands.

4. Alteration in Daily Routine

• Disruption of Routine: Depression may cause a person's daily routine to become irregular resulting in missed meals, poor sleep patterns, and inconsistent exercise routines.

5. Substance misuse

• Self-Medication: Some people may use alcohol or drugs to ease the emotional suffering caused by depression, which can result in substance misuse problems.

6. Agitation or uproar

• Physical Restlessness: Rather than withdrawing from social interactions, some depressed people may display agitation, which is characterized by restlessness and the difficulty of sitting still.

7. Self-destructive or suicidal behavior

• Self-Harm: In severe circumstances, self-harming activities, such as cutting or burning, can be a result of depression. These actions are used to deal with emotional suffering.

• Suicidal Thoughts and Attempts: People with depression are more likely to have suicidal thoughts or attempt suicide, which emphasizes the importance of getting care right once.

8. Modifications in Eating Behaviors

• Overeating or Under-Eating: Depression can result in major alterations in eating behaviors. Some people may overeat to soothe themselves, while others may lose their appetite and lose weight.

9. Easily irritated and hostile

Depression can cause increased irritation and aggressiveness, which can lead to outbursts and disputes with others.

10.Risk-Taking

Some people who suffer from depression may engage in risky activities including excessive spending, risky driving, or harmful sexual practices.

It's critical to recognize these behavioral indicators since they can have an impact on a person's relationships, functioning as a whole, and employment. People with depression can benefit greatly from the encouragement and support of friends and family as they work toward recovery.

When to Get Professional Assistance

1. Persistent Symptoms: It's important to get treatment if depression symptoms last longer than two weeks and interfere with everyday activities.

2. Severe Symptoms: Seeking prompt professional assistance is crucial when depression is severe, indicated by suicidal thoughts or actions, a lack of interest in life, or a considerable impairment in everyday tasks.

3. Recurrent Episodes: Professional assistance can help manage and prevent future bouts of depression if it is recurrent and has several episodes over time.

4. Functional Impairment: When depression severely impairs functioning in areas such as job, relationships, or self-care, it is obvious that help from a professional is required.

5. Physical Symptoms: Physical signs of depression, such as altered sleep or eating habits or unexplained physical pain, should be evaluated by a healthcare provider.

Keep in mind that getting professional help for depression is a show of strength, not weakness. It's a proactive move in the direction of enhancing your mental and emotional health and might mark the start of a path toward recovery, resiliency, and a more promising future. Help and assistance are available, so you don't have to strugglc with depression alone.

CHAPTER FOUR

WAYS TO GET OUT OF DEPRESSION/AVOID DEPRESSION

1. CONTROLLING YOUR THOUGHTS

Being able to control your thoughts is a difficult but important ability that may have a significant influence on your happiness, decision-making, and general sense of fulfillment in life.

The following methods will assist you in having more control over your thoughts:

- **The practice of mindfulness meditation.**

Paying non-judgmental attention to your thoughts and feelings while engaging in mindfulness meditation is a very effective technique.

You may gain more awareness and control over your ideas by simply observing them without attempting to alter or repress them.

Regular mindfulness practice can assist you in separating from unfavorable or bothersome ideas and making the decision not to act on them.

- **Recognize Recurrent Thought Patterns**

Become conscious of thoughts that tend to repeat themselves, such as negative self-talk, catastrophizing, or ruminating.

Keep a journal to document these mental processes as they occur. The first step in taking control of them is to identify them.

- **Challenge Ridiculous ideas**

When you come across negative or illogical ideas, question their veracity.

Ask yourself if there is proof for these beliefs. Are they founded on actual data or suppositions?

Replace negative ideas with more practical and uplifting ones.

- **Establish Time Limits for Worrying**

Set aside certain hours of the day for worrying or attending to worries. Try to shift your focus to more uplifting or useful topics outside of these set periods.

Reduce your time spent worrying gradually to lessen the influence it has on your everyday life.

- **Use Distraction Techniques**

When intrusive or useless ideas come to mind, divert your attention to interesting tasks or hobbies.

Your mental energy can be diverted by engaging in physical activity, artistic endeavors, or just concentrating on a new job.

Affirmations that are positive might be used to dispel unfavorable ideas. These succinct, affirming remarks might help you change your perspective.

If you are thinking, "I'm not good enough," for instance, change it to, "I am capable and worthy."

- **Practice Being Grateful:**

Make a practice of being thankful by constantly thinking back on your life's many blessings.

Positive mental patterns may be changed by concentrating on the things you are grateful for.

- **Limit Your Exposure to Harmful Influences**

Be Wary of Environments, People, or Media that Consistently Encourage Harmful Thoughts.

Limit your exposure to such influences and look for sources that are more uplifting and encouraging.

- **Consult a Mental Health Professional**

If you have trouble controlling your thoughts, feel ongoing anguish, or show signs of anxiety, depression, or other mental health issues, you should seek professional assistance.

Keep in mind that learning to regulate your thoughts takes time, effort, and patience. It's crucial to have empathy for oneself and ask for help when you require it. Gaining the capacity to manage your thoughts may benefit your mental and emotional health, as well as your decision-making and attitude in life.

Activity 1

Get your writing materials

Whatever you think or worry about, pen it down. It doesn't matter how disgusting/irrelevant it is, so long as it makes you worry, write it down. Make it confidential

2. ESTABLISH A PLAN/SET A GOAL

If you want to successfully complete a project or reach a certain goal, making a strategy is essential. A well-thought-out strategy offers focus, structure, and a success road map. Here are step-by-step guide to creating a plan:

- **Set Your Goals**

-Start by stating your goal in unambiguous terms. What do you hope to accomplish? Be very clear and explicit in your goal-setting.

-Set SMART objectives—that is, objectives that are simple, measurable, attainable, relevant, and time-bound. To make your objective more attainable and actionable, make sure it satisfies these requirements.

-Divide your objective into smaller, more doable activities or milestones. This reduces the size of the objective and makes it simpler to monitor your progress.

-Establish a priority list and decide which things you should complete first. Determine which are most important to the accomplishment of your objective and order them appropriately.

-Establish Deadlines: Give each job or milestone a reasonable deadline. This keeps you on track and fosters a sense of urgency.

-Determine the resources you'll need to complete your duties before allocating them. This may involve resources like time, cash, materials, or knowledge. Make sure you can use these resources.

- **Establish a Timeline**

Plan out when you will work on each activity using a timeline or schedule. Regarding the time you can devote to your objective, be realistic.

- **Identify Potential Obstacles**

 Be aware of potential roadblocks or difficulties. Create plans of attack to conquer them.

- **Get feedback**

If your idea entails other people, such as a team or collaborators, get their approval and feedback. Collaboration and communication are essential.

- **Review and Adjust**

Keep track of the development of your strategy. If required, modify the strategy in light of fresh knowledge or novel situations.

To help you keep organized and on top of your responsibilities, use tools like to-do lists, project management software, or a calendar.

- **Monitor and Measure**

Keep tabs on your advancement using quantifiable metrics. This enables you to assess how well you're doing and adjust your course as necessary.

- **Be adaptable**

Be prepared to adapt your strategy if conditions change. To respond to unforeseen difficulties or opportunities, flexibility is essential.

Making a plan is a continuous process, not a one-time event. To make sure you're moving forward and remaining on course while you work toward your goal, always assess and revise your strategy. Keep in mind that a well-thought-out strategy is a potent weapon for making your dreams a reality.

Activity 2

-In your note, write down your goals/dreams

-How do you wish to achieve them

-How is your life going to turn around when you eventually achieve them

3. LIMIT YOUR EXPECTATIONS

Limiting your expectations can be a valuable mindset in various aspects of life. It's important to strike a balance between ambition and realism. Here are a few reasons why it can be beneficial to do so:

- **Reducing Disappointment**

When you set extremely high expectations, you may often find yourself disappointed if reality falls short. By setting more realistic expectations, you can minimize disappointment and negative emotions.

- **Improved Mental Well-being**

Unrealistic expectations can lead to stress, anxiety, and feelings of failure. Lowering your expectations can contribute to better mental well-being as you're less likely to place undue pressure on yourself or others. Relationships are strained when people have irrational expectations. You may promote stronger and more beneficial interactions by having realistic expectations for both you and other people.

- **flexibility**

When faced with unforeseen difficulties or a shift in circumstances, better flexibility is possible due to realistic expectations. You'll be more equipped to deal with obstacles and modify your plans as necessary.

Celebrating Success: When you set realistic expectations, it's simpler to recognize and enjoy even little triumphs, which improves your sense of well-being overall.

Remember, it's not about settling for less; rather, it's about striking a balance between having high expectations and being aware of reality's limitations. A life that is more meaningful and less stressful might result from this balance.

Activity 3

Re-Examine your goal

Are there ones that are hard or goals that are irrationally set?

Are they realistic?

4. KEEP YOUR EGO IN CHECK

A crucial component of preserving mental health and avoiding depression is controlling your ego. Here is why it's important and how to do it:

- **Having a clear understanding of the ego**

 The ego is the mental component of self-importance and identity maintenance. An inflated ego can result in arrogance, defensiveness, and a lack of empathy, despite the fact that it is important for a positive self-image.

- **Depression and Ego**

An overinflated ego tends to make a person too sensitive to criticism, reluctant to change, and prone to unfavorable comparisons with others. These ways of thinking can lead to depression in the long run by fostering emotions of worthlessness and loneliness.

- **Accept Imperfection**

Acknowledge that mistakes and defects are common. The pursuit of perfection is an unattainable ideal that can result in unneeded tension and frustration.

- **Develop a modest Attitude**

Develop a modest attitude by realizing that you are not an expert and that others have significant insights and experiences to share.

- **Accept Feedback**

Be receptive to both critical and positive criticism. Instead of getting defensive, seize the chance to develop and better yourself.

- **Avoid Comparisons**

Constantly contrasting your abilities with those of others might cause you to feel inadequate. Instead of comparing your growth to that of others, concentrate on your own accomplishments and advancement.

- **Develop Empathy**

Empathy enables you to connect with people more deeply. Conflict may be decreased and relationships can be strengthened by understanding their viewpoints and emotions.

- **Give Up Control**

Recognize that there are things beyond your control. Anxiety and frustration might result from attempting to do so. Trust the process and learn to let go.

- **Ask for Help if Necessary**

Don't be afraid to ask for help if you're experiencing sadness or poor self-worth. Counselors and therapists can offer helpful advice and techniques.

Keep in mind that maintaining control over your ego does not imply underestimating your value. It entails realizing that your identity is not exclusively derived from your achievements or how others see you. It's about striking a good balance between ego and modesty, which will eventually improve your mental and emotional wellness.

Activity 4

Engage in Mindfulness Practice, it teaches you to remain in the present moment without passing judgment. This can lessen the power of your ego and increase your awareness of your thoughts and feelings.

Practice Regular Self-Reflection: you do this by evaluating your attitudes, behaviors, and ideas. This can assist you in identifying situations when your ego can be a problem.

5. AVOID PROCRASTINATION AND DISTRACTION

Determine which tasks are most crucial and urgent before giving them a higher priority and Prioritize finishing them.

- **Establish a Schedule**

-Create a daily or weekly plan with designated time slots for each assignment. As much as you can, follow this routine.

-Make a note of the things that need to get done and arrange them according to importance by using a to-do list. To keep track of your progress, check each off as you complete them.

-Create your own deadlines, even for jobs that don't have any. Setting deadlines for yourself makes you feel obligated and helps you avoid putting things off.

- **Reduce Distractions**

Take measures to reduce or get rid of distractions that are frequently present in your area. For example, you may disable notifications, look for a quiet office, or use internet blockers.

- **Create a Productive Workspace**

Designate a space that is suitable for productivity. Make sure it's relaxing, orderly, and distraction-free.

Technology may be a distraction, but it can also keep you focused if you use it wisely. To successfully manage your activities and time, use productivity tools and applications.

- **Use the two-minute rule to your advantage**

If you can do a task in two minutes or less, do it right away. As a result, tiny jobs don't accumulate and become too much to do.

- **Take Breaks**

Include brief breaks during your workday to prevent burnout. Techniques like the Pomodoro Technique, which calls for 25 minutes of concentrated work and a 5-minute break, can be successful.

- **Establish certain periods for Email and Social Media**

Establish certain periods during the day to handle these tasks rather than continually checking your email or social media.

- **Practice mindfulness and meditation**

These practices can assist you in being more conscious of your distractions and refocusing on your current task.

- **Use Visual Aids**

To keep your objectives and obligations in focus, use visual aids like vision boards, sticky notes, and whiteboards.

- **Accountability**

Tell someone who can keep you accountable about your objectives and development.

- **Visualize Success**

Picture the sensation of happiness and success you'll have once you've finished your chores. Visualization is an effective motivator.

Activity 5

-Make a note of the things that need to get done and arrange them according to importance

-Follow the above steps and start doing them one after another

-Write down how you feel after completing each task

6. POSITIVE AFFIRMATION

Positive affirmations can be an effective management and treatment method for depressive symptoms as they promote positive thinking and self-compassion. They can support other therapy modalities and promote mental health.

- **Recognize the Power of Affirmations**

Positive affirmations are comments that highlight your abilities, resiliency, and good qualities. They promote a more positive outlook and counteract negative self-talk.

- **Choose Affirmations Carefully**

Use affirmations that speak to you personally and speak to the particular depressive symptoms you experience.

For instance:

I deserve love and happiness.

"I am powerful, competent, and determined."

"New opportunities for joy are presented every day."

"I'm not a failure."

- **Put it in the present tense**

Affirmations should be written in the present tense, as though the favorable traits or results you seek already exist. The conviction in their actuality is strengthened as a result.

Make affirmations that are good for you a regular habit. Repeat them in the morning, all day, or right before bed Reprogramming your cognitive habits requires consistency.

- **Visualization**

As you continue to repeat your affirmations, see yourself experiencing the world they depict. Imagine what it would be like to have those characteristics or experiences.

- **Write Them Down**

Put your affirmations where you can see them frequently, such as in a diary or on sticky notes. This emphasizes their point and acts as a visual reminder.

- **Think in Them**

In order for affirmations to work, you must sincerely think that they may be true. Develop a sense of conviction and belief in the affirmations you utilize.

- **Customize Affirmations to Your Needs**

Whether it's self-esteem, motivation, or coping with negative thoughts, you may make affirmations that specifically target different parts of your depression.

Positive affirmations are effective when used in conjunction with other self-care techniques, such as counseling, medication (if prescribed), exercise, and a healthy diet.

- **Track Your Progress**

Write down your thoughts and feelings as you employ affirmations in a diary. Keep track of any alterations in your attitude, conduct, or mood over time.

- **Seek Professional Assistance**

Even while positive affirmations may be an effective self-help strategy if you're experiencing serious symptoms of depression, it's imperative that you speak with a mental health specialist. They can offer evidence-based therapies and assistance that are catered to your particular needs.

- **Exercise Patience**

Recovery from depression takes time. Recognize that transformation takes time and practice patience with yourself.

Activity 6

-Have a self reflection, discover your fears and shortcomings

-Turn them into positive affirmation

-Write them down and make sure to look at it all the time

-Don't just recite it, live it. Let your life revolve around it

7. BOOST YOUR SELF-CONFIDENCE

- **Visualize Success**

Envision yourself doing chores or reaching your objectives. Your drive and self-confidence may increase through visualization.

- **Face Your Fears**

Expose yourself to circumstances that test your confidence one at a time. Your confidence increases when you face and conquer your anxieties.

- **Learn New Skills**

Developing new abilities and information might give you more self-assurance. Spend money on training and education that supports your objectives.

Concentrate on your strengths and acknowledge and value your capabilities. Recognize your strengths and use them in many aspects of your life.

- **Maintain Good Health**

Mental health is influenced by physical health. You may increase your confidence by exercising frequently, eating healthfully, and getting enough sleep.

- **Dress with confidence**

Since it can affect how you perceive yourself. Your self-esteem may be raised by keeping a good appearance and attire.

- **Body Language**

Be aware of your own body language. You may convey confidence by standing tall, making eye contact, and making open, friendly movements.

- **Practice Your Speech**

Confidence depends on effective communication. To boost your confidence, practice speaking assertively and clearly, and look for opportunities to speak in front of an audience.

- **Surround Yourself with Positivity**

Spend time with supportive and motivating individuals to surround yourself with positivity. Your self-confidence can be boosted through healthy connections.

- **Accept Compliments**

Be courteous in your acceptance of compliments. Don't minimize your accomplishments or brush off praise.

8. INCORPORATE REGULAR EXERCISE AND A HEALTHY DIET

These are effective supplementary techniques that can raise mood, lessen symptoms, and boost general well-being.

ways a balanced diet and regular exercise might help to treat depression:

- **Increasing Neurotransmitters**

Physical activity increases the release of neurotransmitters including serotonin, dopamine, and norepinephrine. Low levels of these molecules, which are critical for controlling mood, are frequently linked to depression. Essential nutrients that support the generation and function of neurotransmitters can be obtained through a balanced diet.

- **Reducing Inflammation**

Depression has been associated with chronic inflammation. Inflammation in the body can be decreased by a diet high in anti-inflammatory foods, such as fruits, vegetables, and fatty fish. Additionally, regular exercise has anti-inflammatory properties.

- **Improving Sleep**

A balanced diet and regular exercise can both lead to better sleep. Depression frequently causes sleep problems, so obtaining enough restorative sleep is crucial for maintaining mental health.

- **Increasing Energy**

Depression frequently results in exhaustion and decreased energy. Exercise on a regular basis can boost energy and lessen weariness. A balanced diet offers the nutrients required for consistent energy throughout the day.

- **Exercise**

Exercise is a great way to alleviate stress. It encourages the release of endorphins, which naturally improve mood. A healthy diet that contains foods that reduce stress, such as complex carbohydrates and foods high in B vitamins, will help you manage your stress better.

- **Increasing Self-Esteem**

Reaching fitness and nutrition objectives can increase one's sense of worth and self-assurance. Your self-image may improve if you feel more in charge of your health and well-being.

- **Social Interaction**

Taking part in team sports or group exercise may boost social interaction, which is essential for mental health. Depression frequently involves feelings of isolation, and social interaction can offer emotional support.

Diet and exercise may help you build patterns and structure your day. People with depression may benefit from routines because they provide them with a feeling of consistency.

- ## Cognitive Benefits

Depression can affect cognitive function, which includes memory and focus. Physical activity can improve these abilities.

- ## Long-Term Benefits

Developing good habits in terms of nutrition and exercise might help your mental health in the long run. A regular schedule might lower the chance of experiencing depression again.

Activity 7

Make it routine to engage in at least 20 minutes exercise each day

Do not eat rich, eat healthy.

9. MANAGE YOUR TIME EFFICIENTLY

The ability to manage your time well is crucial for success in both your personal and professional life. Factors emphasizing the requirement for efficient time management:

- **Maximizes Productivity**

By managing your time well, you can get the most out of the time that is at your disposal. You may do more in less time by setting priorities for your work and managing your time effectively.

- **Reduces tension**

Anxiety and tension are frequently caused by poor time management. It can be harmful to your mental and emotional health to feel overburdened by a ton of obligations and deadlines. You can regulate your time better and feel less stressed.

- **Enhances Focus and Concentration**

When you effectively manage your time, you may set aside time for certain projects in devoted blocks of time. This laser-like focus can help with concentration and produce higher-quality work.

- **Enhances Decision Making**

Time management helps you assess tasks and come to intelligent conclusions about how to spend your time. Better decisions and more effective resource usage may result from this.

- **Strikes a balance**

Effective time management helps you to establish a balance between your personal, professional, and recreational obligations. Any of these areas that are neglected might result in unhappiness and burnout.

- **Increases Accountability**

When you give yourself clear objectives and due dates, you take responsibility for your activities. Accountability may increase productivity and drive.

- **Improves Goal Achievement**

Your everyday tasks will be in line with your long-term objectives if you manage your time well. It makes sure you're continually making progress toward your goals, which increases your chances of success.

- **Reduces Procrastination**

Poor time management is a common cause of procrastination. Setting deadlines and breaking projects down into manageable chunks will help you resist the temptation to put off crucial chores.

- **Increases Personal Care Time**

A well-planned day makes time for self-care activities including exercise, rest, and hobbies. These pursuits are necessary for both physical and mental health.

- **Increases efficiency**

Efficiency is increased because time management enables you to see inefficiencies in your daily routine and implement the required changes. Time can be saved and productivity can rise as a result.

- **Improves Relationships**

Time spent with loved ones may increase with effective time management. This improves interpersonal connections and minimizes emotions of abandonment.

- **Increases Opportunities**

Time management done well may lead to more opportunities. You're more likely to be given consideration for promotions and career improvements when you're well-organized and reliable.

- **Promotes Work-Life Balance**

Long-term success and satisfaction depend on achieving a good work-life balance. You may dedicate time to both your professional and personal life by using time management.

- **Promotes Personal Growth**

By effectively organizing your time, you open doors for development and self-improvement. You may devote time to education, skill improvement, and following your interests.

Prevents Overcommitment

Good time management enables you to evaluate your capabilities and exercise restraint when required. By doing this, you may avoid taking on too much and make sure you can properly complete your current responsibilities.

Time management is essential for reaching your objectives, preserving your well-being, and leading a full life. It is not merely a practical skill. You may reach your full potential and make the most of your limited time by becoming a time management guru.

10. FORGIVE YOURSELF OF ANY PAST MISTAKE AND LEARN FROM IT

- **Recognize Your Emotions**

Start by recognizing and admitting any guilt, remorse, or humiliation you may be feeling. These feelings are common when you make a mistake.

- **Recognize That Humans Make Mistakes**

Accept that human beings make mistakes from time to time. Everyone makes mistakes in their lives—big or small—because nobody is flawless.

- **Consider the Error**

Spend some time thinking about what transpired. Think about the situation, your choices, and the results.

Consider asking yourself

What caused me to make this error?

What would I have done otherwise?

Were there any warnings or warning signs that I disregarded?

How did my feelings or frame of mind influence my decisions?

- **Accept Responsibility**

Take ownership of your behavior. Owning up to your error is a crucial step in the forgiveness process.

Keep in mind that you deserve mercy and compassion just like everyone else.

- **Challenge Negative Self-Talk**

Be aware of any negative self-talk that may be contributing to your feelings of self-blame. Replace negative thoughts about yourself with positive ones. stating "I'm a terrible person," for instance, is preferable to stating "I made a mistake, but I can learn from it and do better next time."

Learn from Your Mistake: List the takeaways you have from the error. Recognize how you might avoid such circumstances in the future and utilize this information as a chance for personal development

- **Set Reasonable Goals**

Recognize that you cannot change the past. Instead of concentrating on the past, focus on the present and the future by setting reasonable goals for yourself.

- **Seek Others' Forgiveness (If Applicable)**

If your error affects others, think about offering an apology and asking for their forgiveness. Be honest in your apologies, but recognize that not everyone will always accept it.

- **Self-improvement**

Take proactive measures to get better and make corrections. This could entail looking for expert assistance, altering one's lifestyle, or making a concerted effort to better oneself.

- **Gradually forgiving**

Forgiveness is a process that may need some time. Remember to be patient with yourself and that it might not happen right away. Even if you feel like you're making little progress, keep at it.

- **Let Go**

In the end, forgiving entails letting go of the past and letting go of the emotional load brought on by your error. Keep in mind that granting oneself forgiveness is a sign of compassion and love for yourself.

It's a journey, and it might not always be simple, to forgive oneself. It's crucial to put your mental and emotional health first and understand that self-forgiveness is an effective tool for healing and personal growth. You'll progressively develop the capacity to proceed with more self-compassion and a sense of serenity as you complete these tasks.

11. ACKNOWLEDGE AND CELEBRATE YOUR ACHIEVEMENT

Recognizing and appreciating your accomplishments is a crucial habit that improves self-esteem, motivation, and general well-being.

- **Consider Your Successes**

Take some time to consider what you have accomplished, both significant and minor. Appreciate the perseverance and effort that went into earning them.

- **Keep record**

As you grow over time, keep a notebook or record of your accomplishments.

- **Acknowledge the Value**

Recognize the importance of your accomplishments. Take into account how well they fit with your beliefs, aspirations, and long-term objectives.

- **Share Your Successes**

Share your successes with friends, family, and coworkers so that others may join you in celebrating. Sharing your achievements might help you realize their significance.

- **View Successes as Milestones**

Consider your accomplishments as stepping stones rather than your destination. This viewpoint supports further development and advancement.

- **Exercise Self-Awareness**

Make it a habit to appreciate yourself. When you accomplish anything, pause to recognize your effort and perseverance.

- **Give Yourself a Treat**

When you achieve a key objective, reward yourself. A nice dinner, a modest indulgence, or something you've been craving might be it.

- **Extend Your Gratitude**

Appreciate those who gave you assistance, opportunity, and resources that helped you succeed. An optimistic outlook is reinforced by gratitude.

- **Establish a Ritual**

Create a private celebration ritual or custom for your accomplishments. Simple solutions for this include lighting a candle and pausing to think.

- **Keep a Positive Attitude**

Develop a proud attitude toward your achievements. Do not minimize your accomplishments or only attribute them to chance.

- **Take Lessons from Achievements**

Think about the lessons you've taken away from each success. Apply your newly acquired abilities, information, or insights to your next projects.

- **Share Your Success Story**

Tell people about your journey and achievements, especially if it will encourage or inspire them to work toward their own objectives.

- **Keep a visual record**

Record your accomplishments by making a vision board, scrapbook, or digital album. This might act as a continuous reminder of your accomplishments.

- **Set New Goals**

After recognizing a success, set new objectives and tests for yourself. This helps you stay inspired and committed to constant improvement.

- **Honor Others' Successes**

Honoring the successes of friends, relatives, or coworkers may foster a good, encouraging environment that fosters reciprocal celebration.

- **Remain Humble**

While it's vital to recognize and honor accomplishments, it's equally critical to maintain humility and understand that there is always space for development.

Keep in mind that celebrating your accomplishments is about acknowledging your work and strengthening your confidence in your talents rather than boasting or looking for external approval. Recognizing and celebrating your successes on a regular basis may inspire you and increase your drive as you take on new objectives.

CONCLUSION

THE ROAD TO RECOVERY

Overcoming Obstacles and Embracing Hope

Adversity, such as addiction, mental health illnesses, or other life obstacles, frequently forces people to go on the transforming road known as recovery. This route might be difficult and paved with obstacles, but it is also a journey full of chances for development, recovery, and resilience. Let's investigate the fundamentals of the path to recovery, the difficulties it poses, and the optimism it may offer:

Understanding the Recovery Process:

- Acknowledging the Need: Recognizing that change is necessary at the outset of the journey is the first step in overcoming addiction, managing mental health issues, or dealing with other difficulties.

- Commitment to Change: Recovery is built on commitment. Choosing to seek a better, more fulfilled life in spite of the obstacles in your way.

- Self-Reflection: The approach entails in-depth self-reflection to comprehend the underlying causes of difficulties and pinpoint the actions, attitudes, or habits that require modification.

- Seeking Support: Recovering from addiction is a team effort. It frequently entails asking for assistance from experts, friends, family, or support groups who may offer direction, inspiration, and empathy.

- Making a strategy: It's crucial to create a detailed strategy with specific objectives and tactics. This strategy aids in maintaining focus and acts as a roadmap for transformation.

Route Obstacles

Relapses are frequent, particularly in addiction treatment. Although they might be discouraging, they also offer chances to grow and fortify one's commitment.

- Emotional Challenges: Managing emotions, such as anxiety, despair, guilt, or shame, is a crucial component of healing. It is essential to learn how to control and express these emotions positively.

- External Triggers: Triggers might come from outside forces like societal pressures or environmental conditions. Maintaining progress requires creating plans to deal with these triggers.

- Critical Self-Talk: Critical self-talk and self-criticism can be obstacles. It's crucial to develop self-acceptance and self-esteem in order to overcome this obstacle.

- Patience: Recovery is a lengthy process that calls for patience. Even though progress might be sluggish at times, every single movement is a victory

Embracing Hope

- Self-Discovery: Recovery frequently results in self-discovery, enabling people to more fully grasp their strengths, values, and the potential for a happy life.

- Resilience: Surviving adversity builds resilience. It's evidence of one's capacity to persevere and adapt in the face of difficulty.

- Relationships Get Better: As people improve their interpersonal and communication abilities, relationships get better.

- Personal Growth: Personal growth is a key component of the healing process. It provides the chance to develop into a more resilient, self-aware, and compassionate person.

- Hope for the Future: Hope, or the conviction that one's circumstances may change, that one can find pleasure and satisfaction, and that obstacles are not insurmountable, is a crucial component of recovery.

Providing for the Journey

- Professional Help: Consult with therapists, counselors, or medical experts who are knowledgeable about the difficulties you are experiencing.

- Peer Support: Make contacts with organizations or people who have had comparable difficulties. Sharing knowledge and techniques may be very beneficial.

- Self-Care: Give self-care practices like exercise, meditation, and relaxation methods a high priority if you want to improve your mental, emotional, and physical health.

Recovery doesn't happen in a straight line. It is characterized by highs and lows, achievements and failures. However, there is an opportunity for significant change and healing along the way. People may overcome obstacles on their road to recovery by embracing hope, seeking help, and cultivating resilience. As a result, they become stronger, more self-aware, and better able to lead happy lives.

Caption this:

- Create a System of Support: Count on your loved ones and friends for emotional support. Tell someone you trust about your challenges so they can offer support and empathy.

- Challenge negative thought patterns and self-criticism.

- Establish Realistic Goals: Divide your rehabilitation into feasible phases and acknowledge each tiny victory as it is achieved.

- Maintain Consistency: Be kind to yourself and your treatment plan, as well as your self-care routines.

- Establish Realistic Goals: Divide your recuperation into manageable chunks. Celebrate minor triumphs along the road to maintain motivation.

- Stay Connected: Continue to stay in touch with your loved ones. The encouragement of friends and family may be really helpful.

- Take the time to become aware of your depression-related triggers and habits. Recognize the circumstances, ideas, or actions that add to your negative attitude. You may be motivated to take proactive action by this insight.

- Medication Management: If your treatment plan calls for taking medication, consult with your doctor to determine the best drug and dose. Maintain channels of communication open so you may address any side effects or worries.

- Relaxation Techniques: Incorporate relaxation techniques into your everyday routine, such as progressive muscle relaxation, guided visualization, or deep breathing exercises. These can aid in reducing anxiety and tension.

- Consider journaling as a way to maintain tabs on your ideas, feelings, and development. Writing in a journal may be a helpful therapeutic tool for expressing your emotions and seeing reoccurring patterns.

- Join Support Groups: Find support groups or online communities where you may connect with people who have experienced similar struggles and share your experiences with them. Sharing and taking in other people's opinions may inspire and validate you.

- Establishing appropriate boundaries in your relationships is something you should learn to do. To minimize stress and preserve healthy relationships, be clear about your wants and limitations with friends and family.

- Practice Gratitude: Consider the blessings in your life for which you are thankful on a regular basis. This might help you redirect your attention, even under trying circumstances, to the positive elements.

- Keep Up-to-Date: Become knowledgeable about depression and mental health. Making decisions regarding your rehabilitation might be made easier if you are aware of the disease and your alternatives for therapy.

- Maintain your resilience by realizing that setbacks are a typical part of the healing process. Being resilient means having the capacity to overcome challenges. Make the most of setbacks to further your knowledge and progress.

- Encourage kindness and understanding by realizing that healing is a journey rather than a sprint. Be nice and compassionate to yourself, especially on difficult days, and be patient with yourself.

- Celebrate Your Accomplishments: Whether it's a month of regular self-care routines, finishing a therapy session, or reaching a particular objective, acknowledge your accomplishments as you go. These occasions serve to celebrate your advancement.

- Maintain good behaviors: After getting over your depression, keep using the coping skills and good behaviors you've learned. Maintaining a way of living that promotes mental health is essential for avoiding recurrence.

It takes fortitude to overcome depression, which calls for perseverance, devotion, and a dedication to your well-being. Remember that you don't have to face it alone; getting expert assistance and relying on your support system may offer invaluable direction and inspiration. You may overcome depression with courage, self-awareness, and a fresh sense of meaning and joy in life with some time and work.